TEMPERATURE LOG

_____
_____

DEDICATION

This Temperature Log Book is dedicated to all the business owners out there who want to record the temperature of their fridge or freezer and document their findings in the process.

You are my inspiration for producing books and I'm honored to be a part of keeping all of your temperature notes and records organized.

This journal notebook will help you record the details of your fridge and freezer temperatures.

Thoughtfully put together with these sections to record: Equipment, Location, Optimal Temp Range, Contents, Date, Time, Temp C or F, Notes & Comments, Initials, Supervisor Initials, Date & Signature.

HOW TO USE THIS BOOK

The purpose of this book is to keep all of your temperature notes all in one place. It will help keep you organized.

This Temperature Log Book will allow you to accurately document every detail about your fridge and freezer temps.

Here are examples of the prompts for you to fill in and write about your experience in this book:

1. Equipment
2. Location
3. Optimal Temp Range
4. Contents
5. Date
6. Time
7. Temp C or F
8. Notes and Comments
9. Initials
10. Supervisor Initials, Date, and Signature

Temperature Log

Equipment	Location	Optimal temp range

Contents

Entries

Date	Time	Temp C or F	Notes/Comments	Initials

Supervisor

Initials	Date	Signature

Temperature Log

Equipment	Location	Optimal temp range

Contents

Entries

Date	Time	Temp C or F	Notes/Comments	Initials

Supervisor

Initials	Date	Signature

Temperature Log

Equipment	Location	Optimal temp range

Contents

Entries

Date	Time	Temp C or F	Notes/Comments	Initials

Supervisor

Initials	Date	Signature

Temperature Log

Equipment	Location	Optimal temp range

Contents

Entries

Date	Time	Temp C or F	Notes/Comments	Initials

Supervisor

Initials	Date	Signature

Temperature Log

Equipment	Location	Optimal Temp Range

Contents

Entries

Date	Time	Temp C or F	Notes/Comments	Initials

Supervisor

Initials	Date	Signature

Temperature Log

Equipment	Location	Optimal temp range

Contents

Entries

Date	Time	Temp C or F	Notes/Comments	Initials

Supervisor

Initials	Date	Signature

Temperature Log

Equipment	Location	Optimal temp range

Contents

Entries

Date	Time	Temp C or F	Notes/Comments	Initials

Supervisor

Initials	Date	Signature

Temperature Log

Equipment	Location	Optimal temp range

Contents

Entries

Date	Time	Temp C or F	Notes/Comments	Initials

Supervisor

Initials	Date	Signature

Temperature Log

Equipment	Location	Optimal Temp Range

Contents

Entries

Date	Time	Temp C or F	Notes/Comments	Initials

Supervisor

Initials	Date	Signature

Temperature Log

Equipment	Location	Optimal temp range

Contents

Entries

Date	Time	Temp C or F	Notes/Comments	Initials

Supervisor

Initials	Date	Signature

Temperature Log

Equipment	Location	Optimal Temp Range

Contents

Entries

Date	Time	Temp C or F	Notes/Comments	Initials

Supervisor

Initials	Date	Signature	

Temperature Log

Equipment	Location	Optimal temp range

Contents

Entries

Date	Time	Temp C or F	Notes/Comments	Initials

Supervisor

Initials	Date	Signature

Temperature Log

Equipment	Location	Optimal temp range

Contents

Entries

Date	Time	Temp C or F	Notes/Comments	Initials

Supervisor

Initials	Date	Signature

Temperature Log

Equipment	Location	Optimal temp range

Contents

Entries

Date	Time	Temp C or F	Notes/Comments	Initials

Supervisor

Initials	Date	Signature

Temperature Log

Equipment	Location	Optimal Temp Range

Contents

Entries

Date	Time	Temp C or F	Notes/Comments	Initials

Supervisor

Initials	Date	Signature

Temperature Log

Equipment	Location	Optimal temp range

Contents

Entries

Date	Time	Temp C or F	Notes/Comments	Initials

Supervisor

Initials	Date	Signature

Temperature Log

Equipment	Location	Optimal Temp Range

Contents

Entries

Date	Time	Temp C or F	Notes/Comments	Initials

Supervisor

Initials	Date	Signature

Temperature Log

Equipment	Location	Optimal temp range

Contents

Entries

Date	Time	Temp C or F	Notes/Comments	Initials

Supervisor

Initials	Date	Signature

Temperature Log

Equipment	Location	Optimal Temp Range

Contents

Entries

Date	Time	Temp C or F	Notes/Comments	Initials

Supervisor

Initials	Date	Signature

Temperature Log

Equipment	Location	Optimal temp range

Contents

Entries

Date	Time	Temp C or F	Notes/Comments	Initials

Supervisor

Initials	Date	Signature

Temperature Log

Equipment	Location	Optimal temp range

Contents

Entries

Date	Time	Temp C or F	Notes/Comments	Initials

Supervisor

Initials	Date	Signature

Temperature Log

Equipment	Location	Optimal temp range

Contents

Entries

Date	Time	Temp C or F	Notes/Comments	Initials

Supervisor

Initials	Date	Signature

Temperature Log

Equipment	Location	Optimal Temp Range

Contents

Entries

Date	Time	Temp C or F	Notes/Comments	Initials

Supervisor

Initials	Date	Signature

Temperature Log

Equipment	Location	Optimal temp range

Contents

Entries

Date	Time	Temp C or F	Notes/Comments	Initials

Supervisor

Initials	Date	Signature

Temperature Log

Equipment	Location	Optimal Temp Range

Contents

Entries

Date	Time	Temp C or F	Notes/Comments	Initials

Supervisor

Initials	Date	Signature

Temperature Log

Equipment	Location	Optimal temp range

Contents

Entries

Date	Time	Temp C or F	Notes/Comments	Initials

Supervisor

Initials	Date	Signature

Temperature Log

Equipment	Location	Optimal temp range

Contents

Entries

Date	Time	Temp C or F	Notes/Comments	Initials

Supervisor

Initials	Date	Signature

Temperature Log

Equipment	Location	Optimal temp range

Contents

Entries

Date	Time	Temp C or F	Notes/Comments	Initials

Supervisor

Initials	Date	Signature

Temperature Log

Equipment	Location	Optimal temp range

Contents

Entries

Date	Time	Temp C or F	Notes/Comments	Initials

Supervisor

Initials	Date	Signature

Temperature Log

Equipment	Location	Optimal temp range

Contents

Entries

Date	Time	Temp C or F	Notes/Comments	Initials

Supervisor

Initials	Date	Signature

Temperature Log

Equipment	Location	Optimal temp range

Contents

Entries

Date	Time	Temp C or F	Notes/Comments	Initials

Supervisor

Initials	Date	Signature

Temperature Log

Equipment	Location	Optimal temp range

Contents

Entries

Date	Time	Temp C or F	Notes/Comments	Initials

Supervisor

Initials	Date	Signature

Temperature Log

Equipment	Location	Optimal Temp Range

Contents

Entries

Date	Time	Temp C or F	Notes/Comments	Initials

Supervisor

Initials	Date	Signature

Temperature Log

Equipment	Location	Optimal temp range

Contents

Entries

Date	Time	Temp C or F	Notes/Comments	Initials

Supervisor

Initials	Date	Signature

Temperature Log

Equipment	Location	Optimal Temp Range

Contents

Entries

Date	Time	Temp C or F	Notes/Comments	Initials

Supervisor

Initials	Date	Signature

Temperature Log

Equipment	Location	Optimal temp range

Contents

Entries

Date	Time	Temp C or F	Notes/Comments	Initials

Supervisor

Initials	Date	Signature

Temperature Log

Equipment	Location	Optimal temp range

Contents

Entries

Date	Time	Temp C or F	Notes/Comments	Initials

Supervisor

Initials	Date	Signature

Temperature Log

Equipment	Location	Optimal temp range

Contents

Entries

Date	Time	Temp C or F	Notes/Comments	Initials

Supervisor

Initials	Date	Signature

Temperature Log

Equipment	Location	Optimal Temp Range

Contents

Entries

Date	Time	Temp C or F	Notes/Comments	Initials

Supervisor

Initials	Date	Signature

Temperature Log

Equipment	Location	Optimal temp range

Contents

Entries

Date	Time	Temp C or F	Notes/Comments	Initials

Supervisor

Initials	Date	Signature

Temperature Log

Equipment	Location	Optimal Temp Range

Contents

Entries

Date	Time	Temp C or F	Notes/Comments	Initials

Supervisor

Initials	Date	Signature

Temperature Log

Equipment	Location	Optimal temp range

Contents

Entries

Date	Time	Temp C or F	Notes/Comments	Initials

Supervisor

Initials	Date	Signature

Temperature Log

Equipment	Location	Optimal temp range

Contents

Entries

Date	Time	Temp C or F	Notes/Comments	Initials

Supervisor

Initials	Date	Signature

Temperature Log

Equipment	Location	Optimal temp range

Contents

Entries

Date	Time	Temp C or F	Notes/Comments	Initials

Supervisor

Initials	Date	Signature

Temperature Log

Equipment	Location	Optimal temp range

Contents

Entries

Date	Time	Temp C or F	Notes/Comments	Initials

Supervisor

Initials	Date	Signature

Temperature Log

Equipment	Location	Optimal temp range

Contents

Entries

Date	Time	Temp C or F	Notes/Comments	Initials

Supervisor

Initials	Date	Signature

Temperature Log

Equipment	Location	Optimal temp range

Contents

Entries

Date	Time	Temp C or F	Notes/Comments	Initials

Supervisor

Initials	Date	Signature

Temperature Log

Equipment	Location	Optimal temp range

Contents

Entries

Date	Time	Temp C or F	Notes/Comments	Initials

Supervisor

Initials	Date	Signature

Temperature Log

Equipment	Location	Optimal temp range

Contents

Entries

Date	Time	Temp C or F	Notes/Comments	Initials

Supervisor

Initials	Date	Signature

Temperature Log

Equipment	Location	Optimal temp range

Contents

Entries

Date	Time	Temp C or F	Notes/Comments	Initials

Supervisor

Initials	Date	Signature

Temperature Log

Equipment	Location	Optimal Temp Range

Contents

Entries

Date	Time	Temp C or F	Notes/Comments	Initials

Supervisor

Initials	Date	Signature

Temperature Log

Equipment	Location	Optimal temp range

Contents

Entries

Date	Time	Temp C or F	Notes/Comments	Initials

Supervisor

Initials	Date	Signature

Temperature Log

Equipment	Location	Optimal Temp Range

Contents

Entries

Date	Time	Temp C or F	Notes/Comments	Initials

Supervisor

Initials	Date	Signature

Temperature Log

Equipment	Location	Optimal Temp Range

Contents

Entries

Date	Time	Temp C or F	Notes/Comments	Initials

Supervisor

Initials	Date	Signature

Temperature Log

Equipment	Location	Optimal temp range

Contents

Entries

Date	Time	Temp C or F	Notes/Comments	Initials

Supervisor

Initials	Date	Signature

Temperature Log

Equipment	Location	Optimal temp range

Contents

Entries

Date	Time	Temp C or F	Notes/Comments	Initials

Supervisor

Initials	Date	Signature

Temperature Log

Equipment	Location	Optimal Temp Range

Contents

Entries

Date	Time	Temp C or F	Notes/Comments	Initials

Supervisor

Initials	Date	Signature

Temperature Log

Equipment	Location	Optimal temp range

Contents

Entries

Date	Time	Temp C or F	Notes/Comments	Initials

Supervisor

Initials	Date	Signature

Temperature Log

Equipment	Location	Optimal temp range

Contents

Entries

Date	Time	Temp C or F	Notes/Comments	Initials

Supervisor

Initials	Date	Signature

Temperature Log

Equipment	Location	Optimal temp range

Contents

Entries

Date	Time	Temp C or F	Notes/Comments	Initials

Supervisor

Initials	Date	Signature

Temperature Log

Equipment	Location	Optimal temp range

Contents

Entries

Date	Time	Temp C or F	Notes/Comments	Initials

Supervisor

Initials	Date	Signature

Temperature Log

Equipment	Location	Optimal temp range

Contents

Entries

Date	Time	Temp C or F	Notes/Comments	Initials

Supervisor

Initials	Date	Signature

Temperature Log

Equipment	Location	Optimal Temp Range

Contents

Entries

Date	Time	Temp C or F	Notes/Comments	Initials

Supervisor

Initials	Date	Signature

Temperature Log

Equipment	Location	Optimal temp range

Contents

Entries

Date	Time	Temp C or F	Notes/Comments	Initials

Supervisor

Initials	Date	Signature

Temperature Log

Equipment	Location	Optimal temp range

Contents

Entries

Date	Time	Temp C or F	Notes/Comments	Initials

Supervisor

Initials	Date	Signature

Temperature Log

Equipment	Location	Optimal temp range

Contents

Entries

Date	Time	Temp C or F	Notes/Comments	Initials

Supervisor

Initials	Date	Signature

Temperature Log

Equipment	Location	Optimal Temp Range

Contents

Entries

Date	Time	Temp C or F	Notes/Comments	Initials

Supervisor

Initials	Date	Signature

Temperature Log

Equipment	Location	Optimal temp range

Contents

Entries

Date	Time	Temp C or F	Notes/Comments	Initials

Supervisor

Initials	Date	Signature

Temperature Log

Equipment	Location	Optimal Temp Range

Contents

Entries

Date	Time	Temp C or F	Notes/Comments	Initials

Supervisor

Initials	Date	Signature

Temperature Log

Equipment	Location	Optimal temp range

Contents

Entries

Date	Time	Temp C or F	Notes/comments	Initials

Supervisor

Initials	Date	Signature

Temperature Log

Equipment	Location	Optimal Temp Range

Contents

Entries

Date	Time	Temp C or F	Notes/Comments	Initials

Supervisor

Initials	Date	Signature

Temperature Log

Equipment	Location	Optimal temp range

Contents

Entries

Date	Time	Temp C or F	Notes/comments	Initials

Supervisor

Initials	Date	Signature

Temperature Log

Equipment	Location	Optimal Temp Range

Contents

Entries

Date	Time	Temp C or F	Notes/Comments	Initials

Supervisor

Initials	Date	Signature

Temperature Log

Equipment	Location	Optimal temp range

Contents

Entries

Date	Time	Temp C or F	Notes/Comments	Initials

Supervisor

Initials	Date	Signature

Temperature Log

Equipment	Location	Optimal temp range

Contents

Entries

Date	Time	Temp C or F	Notes/Comments	Initials

Supervisor

Initials	Date	Signature

Temperature Log

Equipment	Location	Optimal temp range

Contents

Entries

Date	Time	Temp C or F	Notes/comments	Initials

Supervisor

Initials	Date	Signature

Temperature Log

Equipment	Location	Optimal temp range

Contents

Entries

Date	Time	Temp C or F	Notes/Comments	Initials

Supervisor

Initials	Date	Signature

Temperature Log

Equipment	Location	Optimal temp range

Contents

Entries

Date	Time	Temp C or F	Notes/Comments	Initials

Supervisor

Initials	Date	Signature

Temperature Log

Equipment	Location	Optimal Temp Range

Contents

Entries

Date	Time	Temp C or F	Notes/Comments	Initials

Supervisor

Initials	Date	Signature

Temperature Log

Equipment	Location	Optimal temp range

Contents

Entries

Date	Time	Temp C or F	Notes/Comments	Initials

Supervisor

Initials	Date	Signature

Temperature Log

Equipment	Location	Optimal Temp Range

Contents

Entries

Date	Time	Temp C or F	Notes/Comments	Initials

Supervisor

Initials	Date	Signature

Temperature Log

Equipment	Location	Optimal temp range

Contents

Entries

Date	Time	Temp C or F	Notes/Comments	Initials

Supervisor

Initials	Date	Signature

Temperature Log

Equipment	Location	Optimal Temp Range

Contents

Entries

Date	Time	Temp C or F	Notes/Comments	Initials

Supervisor

Initials	Date	Signature

Temperature Log

Equipment	Location	Optimal temp range

Contents

Entries

Date	Time	Temp C or F	Notes/Comments	Initials

Supervisor

Initials	Date	Signature

Temperature Log

Equipment	Location	Optimal temp range

Contents

Entries

Date	Time	Temp C or F	Notes/Comments	Initials

Supervisor

Initials	Date	Signature

Temperature Log

Equipment	Location	Optimal temp range

Contents

Entries

Date	Time	Temp C or F	Notes/Comments	Initials

Supervisor

Initials	Date	Signature

Temperature Log

Equipment	Location	Optimal Temp Range

Contents

Entries

Date	Time	Temp C or F	Notes/Comments	Initials

Supervisor

Initials	Date	Signature

Temperature Log

Equipment	Location	Optimal temp range

Contents

Entries

Date	Time	Temp C or F	Notes/Comments	Initials

Supervisor

Initials	Date	Signature

Temperature Log

Equipment	Location	Optimal Temp Range

Contents

Entries

Date	Time	Temp C or F	Notes/Comments	Initials

Supervisor

Initials	Date	Signature

Temperature Log

Equipment	Location	Optimal temp range

Contents

Entries

Date	Time	Temp C or F	Notes/Comments	Initials

Supervisor

Initials	Date	Signature

Temperature Log

Equipment	Location	Optimal temp range

Contents

Entries

Date	Time	Temp C or F	Notes/Comments	Initials

Supervisor

Initials	Date	Signature

Temperature Log

Equipment	Location	Optimal temp range

Contents

Entries

Date	Time	Temp C or F	Notes/Comments	Initials

Supervisor

Initials	Date	Signature

Temperature Log

Equipment	Location	Optimal Temp Range

Contents

Entries

Date	Time	Temp C or F	Notes/Comments	Initials

Supervisor

Initials	Date	Signature

Temperature Log

Equipment	Location	Optimal temp range

Contents

Entries

Date	Time	Temp C or F	Notes/Comments	Initials

Supervisor

Initials	Date	Signature

Temperature Log

Equipment	Location	Optimal temp range

Contents

Entries

Date	Time	Temp C or F	Notes/Comments	Initials

Supervisor

Initials	Date	Signature

Temperature Log

Equipment	Location	Optimal temp range

Contents

Entries

Date	Time	Temp C or F	Notes/comments	Initials

Supervisor

Initials	Date	Signature

Temperature Log

Equipment	Location	Optimal Temp Range

Contents

Entries

Date	Time	Temp C or F	Notes/Comments	Initials

Supervisor

Initials	Date	Signature

Temperature Log

Equipment	Location	Optimal temp range

Contents

Entries

Date	Time	Temp C or F	Notes/Comments	Initials

Supervisor

Initials	Date	Signature

Temperature Log

Equipment	Location	Optimal Temp Range

Contents

Entries

Date	Time	Temp C or F	Notes/Comments	Initials

Supervisor

Initials	Date	Signature

www.ingramcontent.com/pod-product-compliance
Lightning Source LLC
Chambersburg PA
CBHW071406080526
44587CB00017B/3189